Western France Travel Guide:

Explore Widely! Brittany, Loire, La Rochelle, Normandy etc. For 2023, 2024 & Beyond. Contains Photos, Best Places to Visit, and Interesting Itineraries. Simply Unforgettable

WELCOME TO WESTERN FRANCE

A land of breathtaking beauty, rich cultural heritage, and warm hospitality, where every corner beckons you to embark on a journey of enchantment and discovery.

Shane Edmondson

Contents

CHAPTER ONE

INTRODUCTION TO WESTERN FRANCE

Why Explore Western France?

Western France beckons travelers with an irresistible charm, enchanting them with its diverse landscapes, rich heritage, and captivating experiences. From the picturesque countryside of Normandy to the rugged coastline of Brittany, and the majestic castles of the Loire Valley to the vibrant cities of Nantes and Bordeaux, this region offers a delightful tapestry of sights and sensations.

A Journey Through Time

Immerse yourself in history as you wander through the cobblestone streets of ancient towns and villages. Trace the footsteps of medieval knights at imposing castles and châteaux that stand as guardians of the past. Explore the well-preserved sites of the D-Day landings, a poignant reminder of the valor displayed during World War II. Western France offers a captivating journey through time, unraveling stories of kings and queens, artists and revolutionaries, that have shaped the nation's vibrant history.

Breathtaking Landscapes

Nature flourishes in Western France, adorning the landscape with breathtaking beauty. The enchanting shores of Brittany beckon with their dramatic cliffs and golden beaches, perfect for tranquil walks and exhilarating water sports. The serene countryside of Normandy, dotted with apple orchards and half-timbered cottages, offers a glimpse into the pastoral charm of rural France. Wander through the romantic vineyards of the Loire Valley, where lush greenery embraces fairytale-like châteaux, creating an idyllic setting for wine enthusiasts and romantics alike.

Cultural Treasures

Western France boasts a vibrant cultural scene that continues to inspire artists and visitors alike. Delve into the world of renowned painters and writers who found inspiration in the region's beauty. Experience the lively festivals and traditional celebrations that showcase the warmth and joie de vivre of the locals. Indulge in the region's culinary delights, from savory crêpes in Brittany to exquisite seafood platters in Normandy, and savor the finest wines from the vineyards that grace the Loire Valley.

Endless Exploration

Whether you seek the tranquility of nature, the thrill of adventure, or the immersion into history and culture, Western France promises an array of experiences to suit every traveler's desires. Embark on a voyage of discovery as you meander through charming villages, explore historic landmarks, and savor the gastronomic wonders unique to each region. Be captivated by the warmth and hospitality of the locals, who take pride in sharing their heritage and traditions with visitors from around the world.

Geographical Overview of the Region

Nestled in the western part of France, this captivating region boasts an astonishing variety of landscapes that will leave any traveler in awe. From the rugged coastlines of Brittany to the verdant countryside of Normandy, and the majestic river valleys of the Loire to the sun-kissed beaches of the Atlantic coast, Western France presents an ever-changing canvas of natural beauty.

Brittany - The Coastal Gem

Stretching along the northwest coast, Brittany showcases a dramatic coastline marked by imposing cliffs, hidden coves, and sandy beaches. This maritime region invites visitors to explore its captivating islands, wander through charming fishing villages, and immerse themselves in its rich Celtic heritage. The rugged beauty of Brittany's landscapes and the invigorating sea air provide a haven for nature enthusiasts and outdoor adventurers.

Normandy - A Tapestry of Tranquility

To the northeast lies Normandy, a land of tranquil charm and picturesque allure. Rolling green hills, apple orchards, and charming half-timbered houses characterize this idyllic countryside. Along its northern border, the English Channel kisses the shores, creating a unique juxtaposition of serenity and maritime history. Normandy's historical significance, witnessed through the D-Day landing sites, adds a layer of depth to this scenic haven.

Loire Valley - The Valley of Kings

Central to Western France, the Loire Valley presents a grandeur of its own with a tapestry of vineyards, fertile plains, and enchanting forests. Often referred to as the "Garden of France," this region boasts an abundance of fairytale-like châteaux, where Renaissance architecture meets breathtaking surroundings. The meandering Loire River provides a serene backdrop for leisurely cruises and leisurely walks amidst lush greenery.

Pays de la Loire - Where Rivers and Oceans Meet

Flanked by the Loire River to the south and the Atlantic Ocean to the west, Pays de la Loire offers a unique geographical blend. Sandy beaches, salt marshes, and wetlands grace the coastline, while the interior reveals a mosaic of fertile farmlands and charming villages. This region is a haven for water-based activities, and its natural beauty beckons travelers seeking tranquility and coastal adventures.

Poitou-Charentes - A Coastal Playground

Located along the Bay of Biscay, Poitou-Charentes entices visitors with its sandy beaches, sun-drenched islands, and diverse wildlife. Embrace the serenity of the Marais Poitevin, often dubbed "Green Venice," as you glide through its intricate network of canals. Poitou-Charentes is a haven for nature lovers, offering ample opportunities for birdwatching, hiking, and enjoying the fresh sea breeze.

Historical Significance of Western France

Steeped in history and imbued with a rich tapestry of cultural significance, Western France stands as a living testament to centuries of human endeavors and momentous events. From ancient settlements to medieval fortresses, and from pivotal battles to artistic movements, the region has played a vital role in shaping the history of France and Europe as a whole.

Normandy - The Epic of D-Day

Normandy's historical significance is deeply intertwined with the momentous events of World War II. On the shores of its iconic beaches, the D-Day landings unfolded on June 6, 1944, marking a turning point in the war. The beaches of Utah, Omaha, Gold, Juno, and Sword witnessed the bravery of Allied forces as they initiated the liberation of

Europe from Nazi occupation. Today, the region pays tribute to this heroic chapter in history through well-preserved museums, memorials, and cemeteries that stand as solemn reminders of the sacrifices made.

Brittany - Celts and Conquests

The history of Brittany dates back to ancient times when it was inhabited by Celtic tribes. Over the centuries, this coastal region witnessed waves of conquests, from the Roman occupation to Viking invasions. Brittany's distinct cultural identity remained resilient, as seen in its unique Breton language and traditions. Exploring its medieval towns and castles, such as the iconic Mont-Saint-Michel, reveals the spirit of a region that proudly embraces its historical roots.

Loire Valley - Castles of Renaissance Grandeur

The Loire Valley holds the crown of France's "Valley of Kings" due to its magnificent châteaux that dot the landscape. During the Renaissance, French nobility and royalty constructed opulent castles amidst the Loire's fertile lands, creating a cultural renaissance and shaping the architectural landscape of the country. The châteaux, such as Chambord, Chenonceau, and Amboise, are not only architectural masterpieces but also bear witness to pivotal historical events and lavish royal gatherings.

Poitou-Charentes and Pays de la Loire - Ancient Roots and Maritime History

These regions, with their strategic coastal positions, have played significant roles in maritime history. Poitou-Charentes boasts a heritage dating back to Roman times, with the city of La Rochelle becoming a prominent maritime trade center during the Middle Ages. Pays de la Loire, too, contributed to maritime exploits with its coastal towns involved in fishing, shipbuilding, and transatlantic trade. Exploring their historic ports and fortifications sheds light on the maritime prowess of Western France.

Cultural Diversity and Traditions

Western France boasts a captivating mosaic of cultures, traditions, and regional identities that enrich the region's vibrant tapestry. As you journey through the diverse landscapes, each area unfolds its unique customs, language, and gastronomy, revealing the essence of its people and their age-old heritage.

Normandy - A Blend of Land and Sea

Normandy's cultural diversity is deeply connected to its geographical charm. The region's inland towns and villages embrace a rustic charm, where locals proudly preserve age-old traditions through folk music, dance, and colorful festivals. In contrast, the coastal communities celebrate their maritime roots with lively seafood feasts and nautical-themed festivities. From the famous Norman cider to mouthwatering Camembert cheese, the culinary delights mirror the region's diverse landscapes.

Brittany - A Celtic Heart

In Brittany, the Celtic heritage beats strongly, reflected in the region's unique language, Breton. As you wander through Brittany's ancient towns, you'll encounter locals donning traditional dress, passionately performing Breton dances, and playing traditional instruments like the bagpipes. Breton festivals, known as "festou-noz," fill the air with joy and camaraderie, celebrating the region's rich cultural legacy. Breton cuisine, with its emphasis on seafood, crêpes, and galettes, captivates food enthusiasts with its distinct flavors.

Loire Valley - The Elegance of Royalty

The Loire Valley embodies a refined elegance that echoes its royal past. As a center of Renaissance art and architecture, the region cherishes its artistic heritage through music, dance, and theater performances. The locals take pride in the Loire's world-class wines, which accompany sumptuous traditional dishes like the famed "rillons" and "tarte Tatin." The grand châteaux, with their opulent interiors and manicured gardens, reflect the aristocratic charm that still permeates the region's cultural identity.

Poitou-Charentes and Pays de la Loire - Maritime Traditions

The coastal regions of Poitou-Charentes and Pays de la Loire embrace their maritime heritage with pride. Fishing villages resound with the rhythms of sea shanties, and maritime museums honor the bravery of local sailors and explorers. These regions' rich maritime past is evident in their cuisine, which features a bounty of fresh seafood delicacies, including the renowned "moules marinières" and "oysters of Marennes-Oléron."

CHAPTER TWO

PLANNING YOUR TRIP

Best Time to Visit Western France

Western France's allure transforms with the changing seasons, offering distinct experiences that cater to different preferences and interests. Each time of year paints a unique picture of the region, from blooming landscapes to festive celebrations and tranquil retreats. Consider the following to choose the best time to embark on your journey through Western France.

Spring - Blossoming Beauty

Spring casts a magical spell over Western France as nature awakens from its winter slumber. The countryside bursts into a symphony of colors, with cherry blossoms adorning the orchards of Normandy and wildflowers carpeting the meadows of the Loire Valley. Mild temperatures and fewer crowds create an ideal environment for exploring historic landmarks and charming villages at your own pace. As Easter approaches, you can witness traditional processions and festivities, immersing yourself in the region's cultural traditions.

Summer - Vibrant Festivities

The summer season exudes a vibrant energy, with Western France basking in warm sunshine and coastal breezes. It's the perfect time to indulge in the region's coastal charms, lounging on Brittany's sandy beaches or exploring the picturesque islands of Pays de la Loire. The Loire Valley's châteaux are even more resplendent amid blooming gardens and festive events. Summer also marks the commencement of numerous music festivals, where the region's artistic soul comes alive with concerts and performances.

Autumn - Harvest and Heritage

As the season transitions, Western France dons its autumn colors, creating a scenic panorama of golden foliage. Vineyards in the Loire Valley come alive with the grape harvest, offering an opportunity to partake in traditional winemaking festivities and tastings. Brittany's coastal towns exude a tranquil charm, perfect for leisurely strolls and savoring seafood delights. Autumn also brings cultural events celebrating local traditions, making it an immersive time to delve into the region's heritage.

Winter - Cozy Charms

Winter casts a cozy spell over Western France, creating an intimate ambiance ideal for exploration and relaxation. The charming Christmas markets in towns like Nantes and Tours emanate warmth and festive spirit. In Normandy, you can experience the allure of the season through holiday traditions, such as the medieval-inspired Christmas celebrations in Rouen. The countryside offers quiet retreats, perfect for sipping hot cider by the fireplace or exploring historic sites without the summer crowds.

Travel Documents and Visa Information

Before embarking on your journey to Western France, it's crucial to ensure you have the necessary travel documents and visa, if required. As a part of France, Western France adheres to the entry requirements set by the Schengen Agreement, which allows for visa-free travel within the Schengen Area for certain nationalities.

Passport Validity: Ensure that your passport remains valid for at least three months beyond your planned departure from the Schengen Area. It's advisable to renew your passport if it is nearing expiration.

Visa Requirements: Citizens of the European Union (EU), the European Economic Area (EEA), and Switzerland can travel to Western France visa-free for short stays (up to 90 days) for tourism, business, or family visits. Additionally, certain non-EU countries, including the United States, Canada, Australia, New Zealand, Japan,

South Korea, and many others, are visa-exempt for short stays in the Schengen Area. However, it's essential to check the latest visa regulations specific to your nationality.

Schengen Visa: If you are a citizen of a country not listed as visa-exempt, you will need to obtain a Schengen Visa from the French embassy or consulate in your country of residence before traveling to Western France. The Schengen Visa allows you to travel within the Schengen Area, including Western France, for a short stay.

Long-Term Visits: If you plan to stay in Western France for longer than 90 days or for purposes such as study, work, or family reunification, you will need to apply for a long-stay visa or a residence permit. The application process and requirements may vary depending on the specific reason for your visit.

Travel Insurance: While not a mandatory entry requirement, it's highly recommended to have comprehensive travel insurance that covers medical emergencies, trip cancellation, and other unforeseen circumstances during your stay in Western France. Having travel insurance provides peace of mind and protects you financially in case of any unexpected events.

Checklist before Traveling

Before departing for Western France, ensure that you have the following documents:

1. Valid passport with sufficient validity.

2. Schengen Visa, if required.

3. Return or onward ticket proving your intention to leave the Schengen Area within the allowed period.

4. Proof of sufficient funds to cover your stay (bank statements, credit cards, etc.).

5. Travel insurance that meets the Schengen Area's minimum coverage requirements, if applicable.

6. Necessary documents for the purpose of your visit (e.g., invitation letters, hotel reservations, etc.).

Packing Tips and Essentials

Prepare for Your Western France Adventure

Packing for your journey to Western France requires a thoughtful approach to ensure you have everything you need to make the most of your experience. From exploring historic landmarks to savoring delectable cuisine, here are some packing tips and essential items to consider for your trip.

1. Clothing:

- **Comfortable Walking Shoes**: Exploring Western France's charming villages, cobblestone streets, and historic sites may involve a fair amount of walking. Pack sturdy and comfortable walking shoes to keep your feet happy throughout your adventures.

- **Weather-Appropriate Attire**: Western France experiences varying weather conditions. In spring and autumn, layering is essential as temperatures can change throughout the day. Summer calls for light and breathable clothing, while winter necessitates warm jackets and layers.

- **Rain Gear**: Be prepared for occasional showers, especially in regions like Brittany and Normandy. A compact umbrella or a waterproof jacket can come in handy.

- **Formal Attire**: If you plan to visit upscale restaurants or attend cultural events, consider packing some formal attire for a touch of elegance.

2. Travel Accessories:

- **Travel Adapter**: France uses European-style power outlets, so bring a suitable travel adapter to charge your electronic devices.

- **Portable Charger**: Keep your devices powered throughout the day by carrying a portable charger.

- **Reusable Water Bottle**: Stay hydrated on your adventures by bringing a reusable water bottle to fill up at water fountains and cafes.

- **Day Backpack**: A lightweight day backpack is convenient for carrying essentials, such as a water bottle, snacks, camera, and guidebooks.

3. Travel Documents and Safety:

- **Passport and Visa**: Ensure you have your passport and any necessary visa documentation securely stored.

- **Travel Insurance**: Carry a copy of your travel insurance details, including the emergency contact number.

- **Money and Payment**: Bring a mix of cash and credit/debit cards. Inform your bank about your travel plans to avoid any card issues.

- **Travel Wallet**: Keep your important documents, such as your passport and cards, organized and safe in a travel wallet or pouch.

4. Personal Care:

- **Sunscreen**: Protect your skin from the sun, especially during the summer months when the sun can be intense.

- **Toiletries**: Pack your essential toiletries, including toothbrush, toothpaste, shampoo, and any personal medications.

- **First Aid Kit**: Carry a basic first aid kit with items like adhesive bandages, pain relievers, antiseptic wipes, and motion sickness tablets.

5. Language and Guidebooks:

- **French Phrasebook**: While many people in tourist areas speak English, having a basic French phrasebook can be helpful and appreciated by locals.

- **Guidebooks and Maps**: Consider bringing guidebooks or downloading travel apps with maps and useful information about the regions you plan to explore.

CHAPTER THREE

DISCOVERING NORMANDY

Exploring the Charming Normandy Countryside

Nestled in northwestern France, the charming Normandy countryside beckons travelers with its idyllic landscapes, dotted with rolling hills, verdant pastures, and charming farmhouses. This picturesque retreat is a haven for those seeking tranquility, natural beauty, and a glimpse into the rural heart of France.

1. The Beauty of Normandy's Rural Landscapes

Step away from the bustling cities and immerse yourself in the tranquil countryside of Normandy. As you traverse the winding country roads, you'll be greeted by vast fields of vibrant flowers, golden wheat, and grazing cows that embody the essence of rural France. Breathe in the fresh air scented with apple blossoms and witness the charm of quaint villages, where time seems to slow down.

2. Half-Timbered Cottages and Storybook Villages

Normandy's countryside is dotted with enchanting half-timbered cottages, their wooden beams exuding a fairytale-like charm. Discover the storybook villages of Beuvron-en-Auge, Lyons-la-Forêt, and Saint-Céneri-le-Gérei, each boasting a unique character and captivating ambiance. Stroll along cobblestone streets, admire well-preserved medieval architecture, and revel in the serenity of these hidden gems.

3. The Art of Cider Making

Normandy is renowned for its apple orchards, and the art of cider making is deeply ingrained in the region's culture. Visit traditional cider farms to witness the cider-making process, from apple picking to fermentation. Sample a variety of ciders, from sweet to dry, and pair them with local delicacies like Camembert cheese and apple tarts for an authentic Norman experience.

4. Camembert and Calvados: Culinary Delights

Indulge in the gastronomic treasures that the Normandy countryside has to offer. Taste the world-famous Camembert cheese, which originates from the village of Camembert. Savor the creamy, rich flavors of this iconic cheese, best paired with freshly baked bread and a glass of Normandy's apple brandy, Calvados. The countryside's farm-to-table cuisine showcases the region's bounty of fresh produce, dairy, and seafood.

5. Gardens and Manors: Timeless Elegance

The Normandy countryside boasts beautiful gardens and stately manors that evoke a sense of timeless elegance. Visit the exquisite gardens of Giverny, where Impressionist painter Claude Monet found inspiration in the water lilies and vibrant blooms. Explore the historic manors, such as the Château de Balleroy and the Château de Vendeuvre, and immerse yourself in the aristocratic heritage of the region.

6. Coastal Gems: Honfleur and Étretat

While exploring the countryside, don't miss the opportunity to visit two coastal gems of Normandy: Honfleur and Étretat. Honfleur enchants with its picturesque harbor, colorful buildings, and art galleries. Meanwhile, Étretat's dramatic cliffs and stunning natural arches provide a breathtaking backdrop for a leisurely coastal walk.

Historical Wonders of Normandy

Normandy is a living history book, where each page unveils remarkable tales of triumphs, tragedies, and pivotal moments that shaped the course of history. From medieval fortresses to poignant World War II landmarks, the region is adorned with historical wonders that captivate visitors with their enduring significance.

1. Mont-Saint-Michel: A Medieval Marvel

Standing majestically on a rocky islet, Mont-Saint-Michel is an architectural marvel that transports visitors back in time. This UNESCO World Heritage Site is crowned by an awe-inspiring abbey, once a place of pilgrimage and scholarly pursuits. Explore the intricate Gothic architecture, spiral staircases, and soaring spires that seem to reach for the heavens. As you wander through its medieval streets, the island's history comes alive, evoking a sense of reverence for the generations that left their mark on this timeless wonder.

2. Bayeux Tapestry: An Epic Embroidery

Unravel the captivating story of the Norman conquest of England through the intricate stitches of the Bayeux Tapestry. This remarkable artwork, dating back to the 11th century, depicts the events leading up to the Battle of Hastings in 1066. Admire the skillful embroidery that brings to life scenes of battles, feasts, and everyday life of that era. The Bayeux Tapestry is not just a historical artifact; it is a masterpiece that connects modern visitors to a defining moment in European history.

3. D-Day Landing Sites: Remembrance and Valor

Normandy's coastline bears witness to the indomitable spirit displayed on D-Day, June 6, 1944. The beaches of Omaha, Utah, Gold, Juno, and Sword stand as solemn reminders of the Allied forces' sacrifices during World War II. Visiting the D-Day landing sites, museums, and cemeteries, such as the American Cemetery at Omaha Beach, evokes profound emotions of remembrance and gratitude for the bravery of those who fought for freedom.

4. Caen: The City of William the Conqueror

Delve into the legacy of William the Conqueror in the historic city of Caen. The medieval Castle of Caen, once home to the Duke of Normandy, presents a glimpse into the region's illustrious past. Explore the Abbaye aux Hommes and the Abbaye aux Dames, two impressive monastic complexes founded by William the Conqueror and his wife, Queen Matilda. Caen is a treasure trove of Norman history, where the echoes of the past resonate through its ancient streets.

5. Rouen: Joan of Arc's Legacy

Walk in the footsteps of the iconic French heroine, Joan of Arc, in Rouen. The city's historic center boasts the majestic Rouen Cathedral, which played a pivotal role in Joan of Arc's trial and eventual execution. Discover the Place du Vieux-Marché, where Joan was martyred, and visit the modern Joan of Arc Church, an architectural marvel dedicated to her memory. Rouen's streets carry the echoes of this heroic figure, reminding visitors of the enduring spirit of Joan of Arc.

Culinary Delights of Normandy

Normandy's culinary treasures are a celebration of its rich agricultural heritage and coastal bounty. From creamy cheeses to savory seafood, the region's gastronomy delights food enthusiasts with its exquisite flavors and traditional savoir-faire.

1. Camembert - The Iconic Cheese

No journey through Normandy is complete without indulging in the world-famous Camembert cheese. Named after the village of Camembert, this creamy, soft cheese is a true embodiment of Norman gastronomy. Savor its velvety texture and delicate flavor, best enjoyed with a fresh baguette and a glass of local cider. Visit traditional cheese farms and cheese shops to experience the authentic production process and the passion that goes into creating this iconic delicacy.

2. Seafood Extravaganza

With its long coastline, Normandy is a paradise for seafood lovers. Feast on succulent oysters from the oyster beds of Cancale or the oyster farms of Saint-Vaast-la-Hougue. Delight in mussels marinières, cooked in a fragrant broth of white wine and herbs. Try the coquilles Saint-Jacques (scallops), plump and sweet, pan-seared to perfection. The region's seafood platters, brimming with lobster, langoustines, and prawns, are a sumptuous celebration of the sea's bounty.

3. Apple Delicacies

Normandy's apple orchards yield not only refreshing ciders but also a plethora of apple-based delicacies. Sample tarte Tatin, a luscious caramelized apple tart, or enjoy teurgoule, a traditional rice pudding infused with cinnamon and baked in an earthenware dish. Sip on a glass of Calvados, the region's apple brandy, crafted through age-old distillation techniques, for a taste of Norman savoir-faire.

4. Andouille de Vire - A Savory Sausage

Indulge in the robust flavors of Andouille de Vire, a smoky and spiced pork sausage from the town of Vire. The sausage is traditionally made by encasing tripe and pork chitterlings in a natural casing and then smoking it over beechwood. Andouille de Vire is a popular ingredient in traditional Norman dishes and adds a depth of flavor to stews and casseroles.

5. Crêpes and Galettes

Experience the delectable art of crêpe-making, a beloved Norman tradition. Sample sweet crêpes, drizzled with local honey or adorned with fresh berries and whipped cream. For a heartier option, try savory galettes, made from buckwheat flour and filled with ingredients like ham, cheese, and mushrooms. Crêperies and bistros across Normandy offer a wide range of these beloved delights, perfect for a delightful meal or a quick snack.

Recommended Itineraries for Normandy

Normandy offers a delightful blend of historical landmarks, scenic countryside, coastal beauty, and gastronomic delights. Whether you have a few days or a week to spare, here are some recommended itineraries to help you make the most of your journey through this captivating region.

1. Weekend Getaway: The Essence of Normandy

Day 1: Rouen and Joan of Arc

- Explore the historic center of Rouen, including the Rouen Cathedral and the Place du Vieux-Marché, where Joan of Arc was martyred.

- Visit the modern Joan of Arc Church, dedicated to the memory of the iconic French heroine.

- Enjoy a leisurely lunch at a local bistro, trying classic Norman dishes like coquilles Saint-Jacques (scallops) and tarte Tatin for dessert.

- Afternoon visit to the Gros-Horloge, an ornate astronomical clock dating back to the 16th century.

- Stroll along the Seine River and discover charming half-timbered houses.

Day 2: Mont-Saint-Michel and Coastal Gems

- Early morning departure to Mont-Saint-Michel.

- Explore the iconic abbey and the winding streets of the medieval village.

- Savor a delicious lunch in one of the island's quaint restaurants, featuring specialties like omelette de la Mère Poulard.

- In the afternoon, head to the coastal town of Honfleur, known for its picturesque harbor and art galleries.

- Take a relaxing walk along the Vieux Bassin and enjoy the maritime ambiance.

- Return to Rouen or choose to spend the night in Honfleur.

2. Four-Day Cultural and Culinary Escape

Day 1: Caen and William the Conqueror

- Start your journey in Caen, exploring the historic center and visiting the Château de Caen.

- Discover the Abbaye aux Hommes and the Abbaye aux Dames, founded by William the Conqueror and Queen Matilda.

- Enjoy a traditional Norman lunch in one of Caen's charming eateries.

- In the afternoon, visit the Memorial de Caen, a poignant museum dedicated to the history of World War II.

- Overnight in Caen or nearby Bayeux.

Day 2: Bayeux Tapestry and D-Day Sites

- Spend the morning in Bayeux, visiting the Bayeux Tapestry and the impressive Bayeux Cathedral.

- After lunch, embark on a D-Day tour to the landing sites, museums, and cemeteries along the coast.

- Reflect on the historical significance and valor displayed during World War II.

- Return to Bayeux or Caen for the night.

Day 3: Exploring the Countryside

- Venture into the picturesque Normandy countryside.

- Visit the idyllic village of Beuvron-en-Auge and enjoy a leisurely stroll among its half-timbered cottages.

- Continue to Pays d'Auge, renowned for its apple orchards and charming countryside.

- Experience a cider tasting and enjoy a meal featuring Norman specialties like Andouille de Vire and Camembert cheese.

- Head to the coastal town of Honfleur for the night.

Day 4: Honfleur and Departure

- Spend the morning exploring Honfleur's picturesque harbor and art galleries.

- Visit the Sainte-Catherine Church, the largest wooden church in France.

- Enjoy a seafood lunch in one of Honfleur's waterfront restaurants.

- Depart from Honfleur or travel back to Rouen or Caen for onward journeys.

CHAPTER FOUR

UNVEILING BRITTANY

Coastal Beauty of Brittany

Brittany, a region blessed with an extensive coastline, is a paradise for those seeking breathtaking coastal beauty and maritime charm. With its rugged cliffs, sandy beaches, and picturesque islands, Brittany's coastal landscapes are a canvas of natural wonders waiting to be explored.

1. Pink Granite Coast: A Geological Marvel

The Pink Granite Coast, located in northern Brittany, is a geological masterpiece known for its unique rock formations. Marvel at the pink-hued granite boulders that seem to emerge magically from the turquoise waters of the English Channel. Take a stroll along the Sentier des Douaniers (Customs Officers' Path), a coastal trail that offers spectacular views of the sculpted rocks, hidden coves, and charming fishing villages.

2. Belle-Île-en-Mer: Island of Inspiration

Famed for its inspiring landscapes, Belle-Île-en-Mer lives up to its name, translating to "Beautiful Island in the Sea." Explore the island's stunning cliffs, sandy beaches, and wildflower meadows. Don't miss the impressive Citadelle Vauban, a 17th-century fortress that stands as a sentinel overlooking the Atlantic Ocean. The island's picturesque harbors and quaint villages provide a peaceful retreat, offering glimpses of Brittany's maritime soul.

3. Gulf of Morbihan: A Sailor's Haven

The Gulf of Morbihan, often referred to as the "Little Sea," is an enchanting inland sea dotted with numerous islands and islets. Sail the calm waters and discover the stunning landscapes of this protected natural area. Explore the island of Île-aux-Moines, known for its sandy beaches and charming village, or visit Île d'Arz, where unspoiled nature and coastal trails await. The Gulf of Morbihan beckons sailors and nature enthusiasts alike with its timeless beauty.

4. Quiberon Peninsula: Seaside Serenity

Jutting into the Atlantic, the Quiberon Peninsula entices visitors with its mix of pristine beaches, dramatic cliffs, and quaint seaside towns. Relax on the sandy shores of Plage de la Grande Plage or Plage de Penthièvre, ideal spots for sunbathing and water sports. Take a ferry to the Belle-Île-en-Mer, the largest of Brittany's islands, for a day of exploration and adventure. With its maritime ambiance and seaside serenity, the Quiberon Peninsula promises a rejuvenating escape.

5. Crozon Peninsula: Wild and Untamed

The Crozon Peninsula, located in western Brittany, offers a raw and untamed coastal landscape. Hike along the cliffs of Cap de la Chèvre and Pointe de Pen-Hir to witness the breathtaking views of the Atlantic Ocean. The peninsula's rugged beauty has inspired numerous artists and writers throughout history, capturing the essence of Brittany's coastal wilderness.

Brittany's Rich Celtic Heritage

Deep-rooted in history, Brittany proudly showcases its Celtic heritage, a legacy that endows the region with a unique identity and a captivating tapestry of ancient traditions. From traditional music to colorful festivals, Brittany's Celtic roots permeate every aspect of life, inviting visitors to immerse themselves in its rich cultural tapestry.

1. Breton Language: The Celtic Tongue

Breton, a Celtic language closely related to Welsh and Cornish, is the heart of Brittany's linguistic identity. Although French is widely spoken, especially in urban areas, Breton remains cherished among locals, with efforts to preserve and promote the language through schools and cultural initiatives. Hear the melodious sounds of Breton as you stroll through villages and participate in local gatherings, a tribute to the region's Celtic heritage.

2. Festivals and Celebrations: An Exuberant Spirit

Brittany's calendar is adorned with vibrant festivals that celebrate its Celtic heritage. Among them, the Festival Interceltique de Lorient stands out as a grand gathering of Celtic cultures from around the world. Held annually in Lorient, this week-long extravaganza features traditional music, dance, and art, providing a window into Brittany's dynamic connections with other Celtic regions.

3. Traditional Music and Dance: A Lively Rhythm

Experience the rhythmic allure of Breton music and dance, which reflects the region's Celtic roots. Fest Noz, traditional dance festivals, showcase the intricate steps of Breton folk dances, accompanied by the stirring sounds of bagpipes, bombarde (a type of oboe), and accordions. Whether as an observer or an enthusiastic participant, these lively gatherings offer an authentic taste of Brittany's Celtic spirit.

4. Ancient Megaliths: Standing Stones and Dolmens

The landscape of Brittany is dotted with ancient megaliths that bear witness to its prehistoric Celtic origins. Menhirs (standing stones) and dolmens (ancient burial sites) are scattered throughout the countryside, shrouded in mystery and folklore. Visit the alignments of Carnac, an extensive collection of standing stones, and marvel at the craftsmanship of a bygone era.

5. Saint Patrick's Trail: A Celtic Pilgrimage

Discover the Saint Patrick's Trail, a symbolic journey that traces the footsteps of the revered patron saint of Ireland. According to legends, Saint Patrick is said to have visited Brittany, leaving his mark at various religious sites and wells. Walk this ancient pilgrimage route, connecting Brittany with Ireland and reinforcing the profound ties between these Celtic lands.

Savory Gastronomy of Brittany

Brittany's culinary landscape is a celebration of its coastal bounty and fertile land, offering a savory gastronomy that delights food enthusiasts from near and far. From succulent seafood dishes to hearty buckwheat crepes, Brittany's cuisine reflects its unique terroir and rich cultural heritage.

1. Galettes and Crêpes: A Brittany Staple

The heart of Brittany's culinary delights lies in its beloved galettes and crêpes. Galettes are savory buckwheat crepes filled with an array of mouthwatering ingredients such as ham, cheese, mushrooms, and eggs. Try the classic "Galette Complète," filled with ham, cheese, and a sunny-side-up egg. For a sweet treat, indulge in traditional crêpes, adorned with sugar, butter, or Nutella. These delectable delights are a must-try for an authentic taste of Brittany.

2. Seafood Platters: A Feast from the Sea

With its extensive coastline, Brittany is a treasure trove of seafood delicacies. Indulge in a "Plateau de Fruits de Mer," a grand seafood platter featuring an assortment of oysters, clams, langoustines, prawns, and crabs, served fresh from the ocean. Pair this extravagant feast with a glass of crisp Muscadet wine for a truly delightful experience.

3. Kouign-Amann: A Buttery Pastry Delight

Treat yourself to the indulgent goodness of Kouign-Amann, a buttery, caramelized pastry hailing from Brittany. Layers of butter and sugar are folded into the dough, creating a flaky and sweet masterpiece. Savor the rich, melt-in-your-mouth texture of this delectable pastry, best enjoyed with a strong cup of coffee.

4. Cotriade: The Breton Fisherman's Stew

Embark on a flavorful journey with Cotriade, a traditional Breton fisherman's stew. This hearty dish showcases an assortment of locally caught fish, potatoes, onions, and a fragrant blend of herbs. Cotriade is a celebration of Brittany's maritime heritage, reflecting the fishermen's resourcefulness and their ability to create delicious meals from the sea's bounty.

5. Breton Cider and Chouchen: Local Libations

Complement your gastronomic adventure with Breton cider and Chouchen, the region's beloved libations. Breton cider, made from locally grown apples, offers a refreshing and slightly effervescent taste, perfectly pairing with Brittany's savory dishes. Chouchen, a traditional Breton mead made from fermented honey, presents a unique and sweet option for those seeking a taste of Brittany's ancient beverage heritage.

Suggested Brittany Travel Routes

Embarking on a journey through Brittany offers a myriad of possibilities to explore its diverse landscapes, cultural gems, and culinary wonders. Here are some suggested travel routes to help you make the most of your Brittany adventure.

1. Coastal Marvels: From Saint-Malo to Quiberon

- **Day 1: Saint-Malo**

    - Arrive in Saint-Malo, a historic walled city with a maritime spirit.

    - Explore the cobblestone streets, visit the Saint-Malo Cathedral, and walk along the ramparts for panoramic views.

    - Indulge in fresh seafood at a local restaurant overlooking the sea.

- **Day 2: Mont-Saint-Michel and Cancale**

  - Journey to the iconic Mont-Saint-Michel and explore its medieval abbey.

  - Continue to Cancale, known for its delicious oysters. Enjoy a seafood lunch in one of the charming harbor-side restaurants.

- **Day 3: Dinan and Dinard**

  - Visit the charming town of Dinan, with its half-timbered houses and medieval ambiance.

  - Cross the Rance River to Dinard, a chic resort town with beautiful beaches and Belle Époque architecture.

- **Day 4: Gulf of Morbihan and Quiberon Peninsula**

  - Explore the Gulf of Morbihan, taking a boat tour to discover its islands and tranquil beauty.

  - Head to the Quiberon Peninsula, known for its sandy beaches and dramatic cliffs.

  - Enjoy a relaxing evening in Quiberon before heading back to Saint-Malo or your next destination.

2. Celtic Exploration: From Rennes to Carnac

- **Day 1: Rennes**

  - Start in Rennes, the capital of Brittany, known for its vibrant atmosphere and historic architecture.

- Visit the Parlement of Brittany, the Rennes Cathedral, and the charming Old Town.

- Experience Breton cuisine at a local bistro or crêperie.

- **Day 2: Vannes and Auray**

  - Journey to Vannes, a picturesque medieval town with a charming harbor.

  - Explore the historic center, including the Vannes Cathedral and the Porte Saint-Vincent.

  - Continue to Auray, known for its picturesque port and quaint streets.

- **Day 3: Carnac and Quiberon**

  - Visit the megalithic site of Carnac, where rows of ancient standing stones create an intriguing landscape.

- Explore the rugged beauty of the Quiberon Peninsula, with its sandy beaches and coastal trails.

- Enjoy a seafood dinner in one of Carnac or Quiberon's seafood restaurants.

- **Day 4: Belle-Île-en-Mer**

  - Take a ferry to Belle-Île-en-Mer, a breathtaking island known for its scenic cliffs and natural beauty.

  - Discover the Citadelle Vauban, the charming village of Le Palais, and the island's stunning beaches.

  - Return to the mainland and conclude your Celtic exploration in Rennes.

CHAPTER FIVE

EXPLORING THE LOIRE VALLEY

Castles and Châteaux of the Loire Valley

The Loire Valley, often referred to as the "Garden of France," is a region renowned for its enchanting landscapes and an extraordinary concentration of stunning castles and châteaux. Embarking on a journey through this fairytale-like setting takes visitors on a captivating voyage through history, romance, and architectural splendor.

1. Château de Chambord: Majestic Renaissance Marvel

The grand Château de Chambord stands as an architectural masterpiece, representing the pinnacle of Renaissance design. Commissioned by King Francis I, the château boasts an awe-inspiring double-helix staircase, attributed to Leonardo da Vinci's genius. Explore the intricately designed chambers, imposing towers, and vast grounds, which exude an air of regal elegance and opulence.

2. Château de Chenonceau: The Elegant Bridge Château

Château de Chenonceau is an exquisite gem perched gracefully over the River Cher. With its iconic arches reflected in the water, the château is often called the "Bridge Château." Marvel at its stunning architecture, elegant galleries, and beautiful gardens. Throughout history, Chenonceau was often owned and influenced by remarkable women, earning it the title of "Château des Dames" (Château of the Ladies).

3. Château de Cheverny: Inspiration for Tintin's Marlinspike Hall

Château de Cheverny's stately façade and pristine grounds inspired the fictional Marlinspike Hall in Hergé's famous Tintin comic series. This well-preserved château allows visitors to step back in time, admiring its opulent interiors, ornate furnishings, and immaculate gardens. Don't miss the daily feeding of the hounds, a centuries-old tradition that still takes place on the estate.

4. Château de Blois: A Testament to French History

Château de Blois stands as a testament to the richness of French history, having witnessed significant events and the presence of multiple royal families. Explore its four distinct architectural styles – Gothic, Renaissance, Classical, and Flamboyant – reflecting the evolution of the château over the centuries. Inside, the château houses a museum that showcases its history and displays art and artifacts from various periods.

5. Château de Villandry: A Masterpiece of Gardens

Château de Villandry is renowned for its breathtaking gardens, meticulously designed to create a harmony of colors and shapes. The Renaissance gardens boast ornamental parterres, vibrant flowerbeds, serene water features, and an enchanting maze. Beyond the gardens, the château's interiors offer glimpses of its past, and visitors can marvel at its opulent furnishings and historic artwork.

Vineyards and Wine Tasting in the Loire

The Loire Valley is not only a haven for majestic châteaux but also a paradise for wine enthusiasts. With its diverse terroir and dedication to winemaking traditions, the region produces a wide array of exquisite wines that tantalize the taste buds and captivate the senses. Embark on a wine-tasting journey through the vineyards of the Loire and savor the rich flavors and aromas that have made this region a renowned wine destination.

1. Sancerre: A Taste of Sauvignon Blanc

Known for its exceptional Sauvignon Blanc wines, the vineyards of Sancerre offer a delightful wine-tasting experience. Explore the picturesque landscapes of rolling hills adorned with vineyards and visit local wineries to sample the crisp and vibrant white wines. Pair your tastings with regional specialties, such as Crottin de Chavignol, a delectable goat cheese that perfectly complements Sancerre's refreshing flavors.

2. Vouvray: Celebrating Chenin Blanc

In the Vouvray region, Chenin Blanc reigns supreme, producing a diverse range of wines from sparkling to sweet. Tour the charming vineyards, and be captivated by the unique characteristics of each wine. A visit to a traditional wine cellar or a tasting at a family-run estate provides an intimate encounter with Vouvray's distinctive terroir and winemaking methods.

3. Chinon: The Essence of Cabernet Franc

Chinon is a wine lover's haven for Cabernet Franc enthusiasts. The vineyards, nestled along the banks of the Vienne River, create an idyllic setting for wine tastings. Discover the nuanced flavors of Chinon's red wines, ranging from light and fruity to complex and robust. Pair the wines with local dishes, such as rillettes and goat's cheese, for a delightful culinary experience.

4. Muscadet: The Melody of Melon de Bourgogne

Muscadet, a coastal region near the mouth of the Loire River, is celebrated for its refreshing white wines made from Melon de Bourgogne grapes. Embrace the maritime influences that lend a unique character to the wines and explore the charming villages of the Muscadet vineyards. Enjoy your tastings with the region's famed seafood delicacies, creating a harmonious marriage of flavors.

5. Anjou-Saumur: A Tapestry of Wine Styles

Anjou-Saumur boasts a rich diversity of wines, from luscious sweet wines to elegant rosés and robust reds. Immerse yourself in the vineyard-dotted landscapes and indulge in the diverse wine offerings. Sample

Coteaux du Layon's honeyed nectar, delight in Anjou's light and fruity rosés, and savor the complexity of Saumur-Champigny's red wines. Each tasting reveals a chapter in Anjou-Saumur's rich wine story.

Idyllic Villages and Towns

Amidst the enchanting landscapes of the Loire Valley lie idyllic villages and towns, each resembling a postcard-perfect scene straight out of a storybook. With their charming architecture, quaint streets, and welcoming ambiance, these hidden gems offer a serene escape from the bustling world, inviting visitors to experience the authentic essence of French countryside living.

1. Amboise: Timeless Elegance

Nestled along the banks of the Loire River, Amboise exudes timeless elegance with its cobblestone streets and historic landmarks. Explore the Château d'Amboise, a regal castle that once served as the residence of French kings. Stroll through the charming town center, filled with artisan boutiques, cafés, and delightful bistros. The panoramic views of the Loire River from the château's terraces are simply breathtaking.

2. Azay-le-Rideau: A Fairytale Setting

Azay-le-Rideau enchants visitors with its fairytale-like ambiance, centered around the stunning Château d'Azay-le-Rideau, perched gracefully on the Indre River. The château's reflection in the water creates an ethereal sight. Wander through the narrow streets and admire the medieval and Renaissance architecture of this idyllic village. Be sure to explore the tranquil Jardins du Château, a haven of greenery and serenity.

3. Chinon: A Medieval Gem

Chinon transports travelers to the Middle Ages with its well-preserved historic district and imposing castle. The Château de Chinon stands majestically on a hilltop, offering panoramic views of the Vienne River and the surrounding vineyards. Meander through the medieval streets, lined with timber-framed houses and charming squares. Savor the ambiance of this medieval gem, which once hosted Joan of Arc and Richard the Lionheart.

4. Bourré: Troglodyte Treasures

Bourré surprises visitors with its unique troglodyte dwellings, carved into the soft limestone cliffs. Wander through the troglodyte village, discovering the fascinating history of these subterranean abodes. Don't miss the opportunity to visit one of the troglodyte wine cellars and taste the local wines, aged in these ancient caves. Bourré's intriguing blend of history and natural beauty makes it a hidden gem worth exploring.

5. Montrésor: A Storybook Hamlet

Montrésor epitomizes the essence of a storybook hamlet, with its charming stone houses, ivy-clad walls, and medieval castle. The Château de Montrésor, surrounded by a picturesque moat, adds a touch of fairy tale allure. Wander along the Indrois River, cross quaint stone bridges, and explore the medieval alleyways. Montrésor's romantic ambiance and architectural splendor evoke a sense of timeless beauty.

CHAPTER SIX

DELIGHTS OF POITOU-CHARENTES

Sun, Sea, and Sand: Poitou-Charentes Beaches

The Poitou-Charentes region, blessed with a scenic Atlantic coastline, offers a paradise of sun, sea, and sand for beach lovers and nature enthusiasts alike. From vast sandy shores to picturesque coves, the region's beaches beckon travelers with their natural beauty, diverse landscapes, and a wide array of recreational activities.

1. La Rochelle: Grande Plage and Beyond

La Rochelle, a vibrant coastal city, boasts several stunning beaches. Grande Plage, situated at the heart of the city, is a popular destination with its fine golden sand and clear blue waters. Embrace the lively atmosphere as you relax on the beach or enjoy water sports. For a more tranquil experience, head to Plage de la Concurrence, nestled near the old harbor, where you can unwind with picturesque views of the city's iconic towers.

2. Île de Ré: A Beach Lover's Retreat

Île de Ré is a beach lover's dream, offering a series of pristine sandy beaches along its coast. Plage des Gollandières and Plage de la Conche des Baleines are among the island's finest beaches, featuring soft sand and dunes. Cyclists can explore the island's scenic trails, passing through salt marshes and quaint villages, before reaching these delightful coastal havens.

3. Île d'Oléron: Nature's Coastal Playground

Île d'Oléron boasts a diverse coastal landscape, with beaches catering to different preferences. Plage de la Cotinière is an ideal family-friendly beach, characterized by its calm waters and shallow shores. Plage des Saumonards, on the other hand, offers wilder surroundings, with sand dunes and pine forests. Nature enthusiasts will appreciate the scenic beauty of these unspoiled coastal gems.

4. Chatelaillon-Plage: Resort Town Charms

Chatelaillon-Plage is a charming seaside resort town that offers a mix of relaxation and recreation. The main beach, Plage de Chatelaillon, stretches over three kilometers, providing ample space for sunbathing, beach sports, and long leisurely walks. The town's Belle Époque architecture adds a touch of nostalgia to the coastal experience, making it an appealing destination for all.

5. Royan: Coastal Elegance

Royan, a stylish seaside town, boasts a series of splendid beaches that exemplify coastal elegance. The Grande Conche beach, with its gentle curve and fine sand, is a favorite among visitors and locals alike. Plage de la Côte Sauvage offers a contrasting experience with its untamed beauty and powerful Atlantic waves, drawing surfers and nature enthusiasts seeking a more rugged coastal ambiance.

Marais Poitevin: The Green Venice

Nestled in the heart of Poitou-Charentes, the Marais Poitevin, also known as the Green Venice, is a mystical waterland that enchants visitors with its labyrinth of canals, lush greenery, and serene beauty. This unique wetland, once a vast marsh, was transformed by human hands into an intricate network of canals and waterways, creating a tranquil paradise for nature enthusiasts and seekers of peaceful escapades.

1. Boat Tours: Gliding Through Nature's Tapestry

Discover the essence of the Marais Poitevin with a boat tour along its enchanting waterways. Step aboard a flat-bottomed boat, locally known as a "barque," and allow the seasoned boatmen, known as "bateliers," to guide you through this water wonderland. Glide gently through a mosaic of waterlilies, reeds, and ancient oak trees, as the bateliers share their knowledge of the marsh's history and ecology.

2. The Green Venice: A World of Biodiversity

Immerse yourself in the biodiversity of the Marais Poitevin, a paradise for birdwatchers and nature lovers. Keep your eyes peeled for graceful herons, elegant kingfishers, and an array of waterfowl that call this wetland home. The marshland provides an essential habitat for numerous species of flora and fauna, creating a harmonious ecosystem that captivates and fascinates all who venture here.

3. Exploring on Foot or by Bike: Nature's Embrace

Discover the Marais Poitevin's hidden gems on foot or by bike, exploring the network of well-marked trails that wind through the marsh. Wander along picturesque paths bordered by colorful wildflowers, and pause at observation points to admire the serene beauty of the wetland. The peacefulness and tranquility of the Marais Poitevin create an inviting space for contemplation and connection with nature.

4. Coulon: The Heart of the Marais Poitevin

Coulon, often referred to as the "capital" of the Marais Poitevin, is a charming village that beckons visitors to explore its quaint streets and picturesque canals. Stroll along the banks of the Sèvre Niortaise River, and bask in the charm of Coulon's traditional houses adorned with colorful flowers. Indulge in delicious regional cuisine at waterside restaurants, savoring the flavors of the marsh's bounty.

5. The Abbeys: Echoes of History

In addition to its natural splendor, the Marais Poitevin boasts a rich historical heritage. Visit the ancient abbeys scattered throughout the wetland, such as the Abbaye de Maillezais and Abbaye de Nieul-sur-l'Autise. These timeless structures, surrounded by the marsh's tranquil landscapes, offer a glimpse into the region's religious and architectural history.

Gastronomic Journey through Poitou-Charentes

Embark on a gastronomic journey through Poitou-Charentes, a region that tantalizes taste buds with its rich culinary heritage and delectable delights. From succulent seafood to indulgent cheeses and renowned wines, Poitou-Charentes offers a feast of flavors that celebrates the bounty of the land and the sea.

1. Seafood Delights: Oysters and Mussels

With its extensive coastline, Poitou-Charentes is a seafood lover's paradise. Indulge in the region's renowned oysters, brimming with freshness and flavor, and paired perfectly with a glass of chilled Muscadet wine. The mussels of Charron, plump and succulent, are a true delicacy, often served in a savory broth with a sprinkling of parsley and garlic.

2. Charentais Melon: A Sweet Summer Treat

The Charentais melon, celebrated for its sweetness and aromatic flavor, is a summer treat that delights locals and visitors alike. Savor its juicy flesh, whether fresh from the market or as part of a refreshing fruit salad. Pair it with the region's famous Pineau des Charentes, a fortified wine made from fresh grape must and Cognac.

3. Goat Cheese: Crottin de Chavignol

Poitou-Charentes boasts a tradition of exceptional goat cheese, with Crottin de Chavignol standing out as a local gem. These small, creamy cheeses are produced with meticulous care by local farmers, resulting in a delightful balance of flavors. Savor Crottin de Chavignol on its own or add it to salads and warm dishes for a burst of gastronomic pleasure.

4. Poitou-Charentes Butter: A Taste of Terroir

The butter of Poitou-Charentes is renowned for its high quality and distinct taste. Made from the milk of cows grazing on the region's lush pastures, this golden-hued butter is a testament to the land's rich terroir. Spread it generously on freshly baked bread or use it as a flavorful base for cooking traditional French dishes.

5. Cognac: A World of Refined Spirits

Poitou-Charentes is home to the famous Cognac, a globally celebrated brandy known for its sophistication and complexity. Explore the vineyards and distilleries, learning about the intricate process of Cognac production. Sip on a range of Cognac varieties, from VS (Very Special) to XO (Extra Old), experiencing the elegance and finesse of this prized spirit.

CHAPTER SEVEN

COASTAL CHARMS OF PAYS DE LA LOIRE

Atlantic Coast Highlights

The Atlantic Coast of France is a mesmerizing playground that beckons travelers with its stunning landscapes, picturesque beaches, and captivating coastal towns. From the majestic cliffs to the sandy shores, the Atlantic Coast boasts a myriad of highlights that promise unforgettable experiences for every type of adventurer.

1. Biarritz: A Surfing Haven

Biarritz, nestled along the Basque coast, is a vibrant seaside town renowned for its world-class surfing conditions. The waves of La Grande Plage and Côte des Basques attract surfers from around the globe, while the elegant architecture and Belle Époque charm of Biarritz add an air of sophistication. Stroll along the waterfront, breathe in the salty ocean breeze, and immerse yourself in the surf culture of this lively coastal gem.

2. La Rochelle: Maritime Magic

La Rochelle, an enchanting maritime city, is a captivating blend of history and coastal beauty. The Old Port, guarded by iconic medieval towers, exudes an atmosphere of timeless elegance. Explore the picturesque streets lined with historic buildings and enjoy the lively ambiance of the city's quays and cafés. Don't miss a visit to the Aquarium La Rochelle, where you can get up close to marine life from the Atlantic Ocean.

3. Arcachon: Dune du Pilat and Oyster Delights

Arcachon, nestled on the shores of the Arcachon Bay, offers a captivating natural landscape and a culinary delight. Climb the majestic Dune du Pilat, the tallest sand dune in Europe, for breathtaking views of the bay and the surrounding pine forests. Indulge in the region's famed oysters, freshly harvested from the bay, and enjoy them with a glass of crisp white wine.

4. Île de Ré: Tranquil Island Beauty

Île de Ré, a serene island off the coast of La Rochelle, is a haven of tranquility and natural beauty. Discover the island's picturesque villages with their white-washed houses adorned with hollyhocks. Cycle along the network of bike paths, exploring salt marshes, sandy beaches, and lush vineyards. Enjoy fresh seafood at charming seaside restaurants, savoring the flavors of the Atlantic.

5. Cap Ferret: Laid-Back Seaside Retreat

Cap Ferret, a laid-back seaside retreat on the Arcachon Bay, entices visitors with its unspoiled landscapes and relaxed ambiance. Wander along the stunning beaches, bask in the sun, and savor the laid-back atmosphere of this charming coastal haven. Don't miss the chance to savor the renowned oysters of Cap Ferret, a culinary delight that complements the coastal experience.

Nantes: A Vibrant City by the River

Nantes, a vibrant city in western France, exudes a captivating blend of history, culture, and modernity. Situated along the banks of the Loire River, this dynamic metropolis offers a plethora of attractions, lively neighborhoods, and a creative spirit that has earned it the reputation as a cultural hub.

1. Château des Ducs de Bretagne: A Royal Legacy

At the heart of Nantes stands the impressive Château des Ducs de Bretagne, a symbol of the city's historical significance. This magnificent castle served as the residence of the Dukes of Brittany and offers a fascinating journey through time. Explore the fortress's towers, ramparts, and exhibition rooms that recount the region's rich heritage. The castle's picturesque courtyard hosts various cultural events throughout the year.

2. Les Machines de l'île: A Steampunk Wonderland

Step into a world of imagination and wonder at Les Machines de l'île, an extraordinary artistic project that blends steampunk aesthetics and mechanical marvels. Marvel at the Grand Elephant, a gigantic mechanical elephant that roams the streets with passengers on its back. The Carousel of the Marine Worlds, a stunning work of art, invites visitors to ride whimsical marine-themed creatures.

3. Île de Nantes: Urban Renewal and Creativity

Île de Nantes, once an industrial site, has undergone a transformation into a hub of creativity and urban renewal. Explore the creative and quirky architectural designs that now grace the island, such as the famous "Maison dans la Loire," a house seemingly floating on the river. The island is a hotspot for art galleries, cultural events, and street art, reflecting Nantes' dynamic and artistic spirit.

4. Passage Pommeraye: Timeless Elegance

Indulge in a shopping experience like no other at Passage Pommeraye, an elegant 19th-century shopping arcade. This architectural gem boasts a stunning glass roof, ornate staircases, and charming boutiques that transport visitors to a bygone era of sophistication and refinement. Take a leisurely stroll through the passage, admiring its timeless beauty and boutique offerings.

5. Erdre River: Serenity and Green Spaces

Escape the urban bustle and find serenity along the tranquil Erdre River, known as the "most beautiful river in France." Rent a boat or join a river cruise to explore the verdant landscapes and elegant châteaux lining the riverbanks. The Parc de Procé, a lush park with meandering paths and enchanting gardens, offers a peaceful retreat for leisurely walks and picnics.

Nature and Wildlife in Pays de la Loire

Pays de la Loire, nestled in the western part of France, boasts a diverse and enchanting landscape that offers a haven for nature enthusiasts and wildlife lovers alike. From picturesque coastlines to lush forests, serene lakes, and protected wetlands, the region's natural beauty beckons travelers to explore its bountiful biodiversity.

1. Brière Regional Natural Park: Wetland Wonder

The Brière Regional Natural Park, a sprawling wetland encompassing marshes, canals, and ponds, is a paradise for birdwatchers and nature lovers. Embark on a boat tour to glide through the marshy waters, catching glimpses of graceful herons, vibrant kingfishers, and other waterfowl. The park's thatched-roof cottages add to its charm, offering a glimpse into traditional rural life.

2. Puy du Fou: Nature and History Unite

Puy du Fou, a unique theme park that celebrates history and nature, is a remarkable journey through time. Spectacular shows and reenactments showcase historical events, surrounded by lush greenery and picturesque landscapes. Discover themed gardens, ancient forests, and serene lakes that blend seamlessly with the park's captivating performances.

3. Île d'Yeu: Coastal Beauty

Île d'Yeu, a scenic island off the Vendée coast, captivates visitors with its rugged coastline, sandy beaches, and azure waters. Explore the island's coastal paths, meandering through rugged cliffs and lush vegetation, offering panoramic views of the Atlantic Ocean. Birdwatchers will be delighted by the island's diverse avian inhabitants, including seabird colonies that dot the cliffs.

4. Marais Poitevin: The Green Venice

As mentioned earlier, the Marais Poitevin, also known as the Green Venice, offers a mystical journey through marshes and canals. Navigate the peaceful waterways, surrounded by lush vegetation, and immerse yourself in the region's serene beauty. The marshland is home to a rich variety of flora and fauna, making it a sanctuary for nature enthusiasts.

5. Forêt de Bercé: Majestic Woodland

The Forêt de Bercé, a majestic forest near Le Mans, is a sanctuary of tranquility and natural splendor. Walk through its towering beech and oak trees, and breathe in the fresh forest air. The forest is home to an array of wildlife, including deer, wild boars, and various bird species, making it a delightful destination for wildlife observation.

CHAPTER EIGHT

BRITTANY'S ATLANTIC COASTLINE

Seaside Retreats in Southern Brittany

Southern Brittany beckons travelers with its picturesque coastline, dotted with charming seaside retreats that offer a perfect blend of relaxation, outdoor activities, and coastal allure. From golden sandy beaches to rugged cliffs and serene coves, the region's coastal towns and villages invite visitors to immerse themselves in the beauty of the Atlantic Ocean.

1. Quiberon: A Peninsula Paradise

Quiberon, a stunning peninsula jutting into the Atlantic, is a true paradise for beach lovers and water sports enthusiasts. Its long stretches of sandy beaches, such as the Grande Plage and Plage de Port Maria, offer ideal spots for sunbathing and swimming. Adventure seekers can try their hand at wind and kite surfing, while nature lovers will appreciate the diverse marine life and birdwatching opportunities.

2. Belle-Île-en-Mer: Natural Beauty Unleashed

Belle-Île-en-Mer, the largest of Brittany's islands, lives up to its name as a "beautiful island at sea." Its rugged coastline, dramatic cliffs, and hidden coves create a picturesque setting for exploration. The beach of Les Grands Sables, with its unique shell-shaped formation, is a must-visit. Delve into the island's charming villages, such as Le Palais and Sauzon, and discover the island's artistic heritage that inspired renowned painter Claude Monet.

3. Carnac: Megalithic Marvels

Carnac, famous for its megalithic alignments, is a coastal town that marries history with natural beauty. Explore the mysterious standing stones that date back to prehistoric times and ponder their enigmatic significance. Carnac's beaches, including the Grande Plage and Plage de Légenèse, offer delightful spots for family-friendly beach days and water-based activities.

4. La Baule-Escoublac: Belle Époque Elegance

La Baule-Escoublac, known for having one of the most beautiful beaches in Europe, exudes belle époque elegance and sophistication. The three-kilometer-long sandy beach, bordered by elegant hotels and villas, provides a scenic backdrop for leisurely strolls and sun-soaked afternoons. The beachfront promenade, lively with cafes and boutiques, offers a vibrant ambiance to savor.

5. Concarneau: A Walled Seaside Gem

Concarneau, a fortified town on the coast, captivates visitors with its medieval charm and maritime allure. Stroll through the historic Ville Close, a walled citadel built on a rocky islet, and admire the charming fishing port within. The nearby Plage des Sables Blancs and Plage de Cornouaille offer tranquil spots to relax and enjoy views of the picturesque harbor.

Surfing and Water Sports Hotspots

Southern Brittany's Atlantic coastline offers a thrilling playground for surfers and water sports enthusiasts, attracting adrenaline-seekers to its diverse range of surfing and aquatic activities. Whether you're a seasoned pro or a beginner looking to catch your first wave, the region's hotspots promise exhilarating experiences on the water.

1. Quiberon Peninsula: Surfing Haven

The Quiberon Peninsula is a mecca for surfers, boasting a variety of breaks suitable for all skill levels. Experienced surfers will relish the challenge of the legendary "La Côte Sauvage," where powerful waves crash against the rocky coastline. Beginners can head to the sheltered beaches of Plage de Penthièvre or Plage de la Grande Plage for gentler waves and surfing lessons.

2. La Torche: Surfing and Windsurfing Paradise

La Torche, located in the Finistère department, is renowned for its exceptional surfing and windsurfing conditions. This exposed stretch of coast catches the full force of Atlantic swells, creating world-class waves for surfers seeking thrills. The consistent winds make it an ideal spot for windsurfers to glide across the water and perform impressive maneuvers.

3. Belle-Île-en-Mer: Ocean Adventures

Belle-Île-en-Mer not only captivates with its natural beauty but also offers an array of water sports opportunities. Kayaking and paddleboarding enthusiasts will find calm waters along the island's sheltered coves, providing a chance to explore the coastline and hidden sea caves. For a more adventurous experience, join snorkeling excursions to discover the island's vibrant underwater world.

4. Crozon Peninsula: Diverse Watersports Playground

The Crozon Peninsula, located in the Armorique Natural Regional Park, caters to water sports enthusiasts of all kinds. Surfers can catch waves at various beaches, including the popular Goulien Beach and Lostmarc'h Beach. The sheltered coves are perfect for kayaking and stand-up paddleboarding, while divers can explore the intriguing underwater wrecks and marine life.

5. Lesconil: Sailing and Kite Surfing Delight

Lesconil, a charming fishing village, is a hidden gem for sailing and kite surfing aficionados. The steady sea breezes create an idyllic environment for sailing enthusiasts to set sail and explore the scenic coast. Kite surfers can take advantage of the open beaches and favorable wind conditions, providing ample opportunities to ride the waves and perform aerial tricks.

Lighthouses and Maritime Heritage

Southern Brittany is adorned with iconic lighthouses that stand as beacons of maritime heritage, guiding sailors and illuminating the region's rich nautical history. These majestic structures not only serve as functional navigational aids but also hold captivating stories of seafaring adventures and maritime traditions.

1. Phare d'Eckmühl: Majestic Maritime Sentinel

The Phare d'Eckmühl, perched on the rocky headland of Pointe de Penmarc'h, is one of the most majestic lighthouses in Brittany. Named after the Duchess of Westminster, the lighthouse rises 65 meters above the sea, offering breathtaking views of the rugged coastline and the Atlantic Ocean. A climb to the top rewards visitors with panoramic vistas and a glimpse into the lighthouse's fascinating history.

2. Phare de Portzic: Preserving Naval Heritage

The Phare de Portzic, situated on the Goulet de Brest, plays a vital role in preserving Brittany's naval heritage. This historic lighthouse, with its distinctive black and white stripes, was once a guide for naval convoys entering the Brest harbor. Today, it stands as a symbol of maritime pride and is open to the public, offering visitors a chance to learn about the region's maritime history.

3. Phare du Petit Minou: A Romantic Seaside Icon

The Phare du Petit Minou, located at the entrance of the Brest harbor, stands as a romantic sentinel on the rocky cliffs. This picturesque lighthouse, painted in white and red stripes, offers an idyllic setting for walks along the coastal path. As night falls, witness the lighthouse's beam illuminating the dark waters, reminiscent of timeless tales of seafaring voyages.

4. Phare du Grand Jardin: A Coastal Guardian

The Phare du Grand Jardin, situated on Île de Groix, watches over the maritime traffic and marks the entrance to the harbor of Lorient. With its unique square tower, this lighthouse exudes a sense of coastal guardianship. The island's maritime museum offers visitors an opportunity to delve into the island's seafaring history and the role of the lighthouse in safeguarding ships.

5. Phare de la Teignouse: Secluded Seafarer's Haven

The Phare de la Teignouse, located on a remote rocky islet, is an isolated seafarer's haven that stands strong against the crashing waves. This quaint lighthouse, accessible only by boat, captivates with its solitary charm and the wild beauty of its surroundings. Embark on a boat excursion to witness the lighthouse's fascinating isolation and hear tales of its maritime significance.

CHAPTER NINE

EMBRACING LOCAL CULTURE

Language and Useful Phrases

While visiting Southern Brittany, embracing a few basic French phrases can enhance your travel experience and foster connections with locals. French is the official language, and although many people in tourist areas may speak English, making an effort to communicate in French is appreciated and shows cultural respect.

1. Greetings and Polite Expressions

- **Bonjour (bohn-zhoor)** - Hello / Good day

- **Bonsoir (bohn-swahr)** - Good evening

- **Merci (mehr-see)** - Thank you

- **S'il vous plaît (seel voo pleh)** - Please

- **Excusez-moi (ehk-skew-zay mwa)** - Excuse me / Pardon me

2. Basic Conversational Phrases

- **Comment ça va ? (koh-mahn sah vah)** - How are you?

- **Oui (wee)** - Yes

- **Non (noh)** - No

- **Je ne parle pas français (zhuh nuh parl pah frahn-seh)** - I don't speak French

- **Parlez-vous anglais ? (par-leh voo ahn-gleh ?)** - Do you speak English?

3. Ordering Food and Drinks

- **Une table pour deux, s'il vous plaît (ewn tahbl poor duh, seel voo pleh)** - A table for two, please

- **La carte, s'il vous plaît (lah kart, seel voo pleh)** - The menu, please

- **L'addition, s'il vous plaît (lah-dee-syon, seel voo pleh)** - The bill, please

- **Je voudrais... (zhuh voo-dreh...)** - I would like...

- **L'eau (loh)** - Water

- **Vin rouge / blanc (van roozh / blahn)** - Red wine / White wine

- **Une baguette, s'il vous plaît (ewn bah-get, seel voo pleh)** - A baguette, please

4. Asking for Directions

- **Où est... ? (oo eh... ?)** - Where is... ?

- **La plage (lah plahzh)** - The beach

- **La gare (lah gah-r)** - The train station

- **L'hôtel (loh-tel)** - The hotel

- **Le restaurant (luh reh-stoh-rahn)** - The restaurant

- **À gauche (ah gohsh)** - To the left

- **À droite (ah drwaht)** - To the right

- **Tout droit (too drwah)** - Straight ahead

Traditional Festivals and Celebrations

Southern Brittany celebrates its rich cultural heritage with a tapestry of traditional festivals and vibrant celebrations that showcase the region's history, folklore, and sense of community. These colorful events bring locals and visitors together in a joyful display of customs, music, dance, and gastronomy, providing a unique insight into the cultural soul of the region.

1. Fest-Noz: Breton Folk Dancing

Fest-Noz is a lively celebration of Breton folk music and dance, where locals and visitors come together to enjoy an evening of dancing, singing, and merrymaking. Traditional Breton instruments, such as the accordion, bombarde, and bagpipes, provide the musical backdrop for the energetic and intricate dance performances. Fest-Noz is an excellent opportunity to immerse yourself in Breton culture, connect with locals, and experience the joy of community gatherings.

2. Fête des Filets Bleus: Celebrating Coastal Heritage

The Fête des Filets Bleus, held in Concarneau, pays homage to the town's maritime heritage and fishing traditions. This lively festival features colorful parades, folk performances, and artisanal craft markets. The highlight is the "filets bleus" (blue nets) worn by the locals, which symbolize the town's seafaring identity. Savor delicious seafood dishes, join in the festive atmosphere, and explore the maritime charm of Concarneau.

3. Festival Interceltique de Lorient: Celtic Showcase

The Festival Interceltique de Lorient is a major event that celebrates Celtic cultures from around the world. Held in the city of Lorient, the festival brings together musicians, dancers, and artists from Brittany, Scotland, Ireland, Wales, Galicia, and beyond. Enjoy captivating performances of traditional music, witness impressive Celtic dance displays, and partake in the vibrant festivities that celebrate the shared heritage of Celtic nations.

4. Festival de Cornouaille: Breton Pride

The Festival de Cornouaille, held in Quimper, is a lively celebration of Breton culture and pride. Traditional Breton costumes, music, and dance performances fill the streets with color and energy. The festival features various competitions, including Breton music and dance contests, providing a platform for talented artists to showcase their skills. Explore the artistic and culinary traditions of Brittany, and experience the warm hospitality of the locals.

5. Festival du Bout du Monde: World Music Extravaganza

The Festival du Bout du Monde, held in Crozon, is a musical extravaganza that celebrates world music and cultural diversity. Musicians from different corners of the globe come together to perform a diverse range of music genres, creating a unique and harmonious fusion of sounds. This festival promotes cultural exchange, encourages dialogue among cultures, and fosters a spirit of unity and understanding.

Arts, Crafts, and Music in the Region

Southern Brittany's vibrant arts, crafts, and music scene showcases the region's rich cultural heritage and artistic spirit. From traditional crafts passed down through generations to contemporary artistic expressions, the region offers a kaleidoscope of creativity that captivates the senses and reflects the soul of its people.

1. Breton Artistry: Peinture et Sculpture

Breton artistry encompasses a diverse range of painting and sculpture, often inspired by the region's natural beauty, folklore, and maritime heritage. Local artists create stunning pieces that capture the essence of Brittany, from picturesque landscapes to vibrant depictions of Breton life. Art galleries and exhibitions throughout the region provide an opportunity to admire and collect these unique works of art.

2. Pottery and Ceramics: An Artisan Tradition

Pottery and ceramics hold a special place in Breton artisan traditions. Quimper, renowned for its faience pottery, produces exquisitely hand-painted pieces that feature intricate floral motifs and Breton folk designs. Visitors can explore workshops and boutiques to witness skilled artisans crafting these beautiful and functional pieces that serve as cherished souvenirs of the region.

3. Traditional Music: Son et Danse Bretonne

Southern Brittany is steeped in the tradition of Breton music, which forms an integral part of the region's cultural identity. The distinct sound of traditional Breton instruments, including the bombard, biniou, and diatonic accordion, enlivens festivals and gatherings. Fest-Noz, mentioned earlier, offers a splendid opportunity to experience the captivating rhythm and joyous dances of Breton music.

4. Festivals of Art and Music

Throughout the year, Southern Brittany hosts a multitude of festivals that celebrate the arts and music. The Festival Interceltique de Lorient, as mentioned before, brings together Celtic music and performances from various countries. Additionally, the Festival de Cornouaille highlights Breton music, dance, and crafts, drawing artists and visitors from all corners of the region.

5. Contemporary Art and Cultural Events

In addition to traditional arts, Southern Brittany embraces contemporary art and cultural events. Numerous art galleries, cultural centers, and music venues showcase the works of local and international artists. From exhibitions and performances to street art and live concerts, the region offers a dynamic and eclectic cultural scene that appeals to art enthusiasts and creative minds alike.

CHAPTER TEN

PRACTICAL TRAVEL INFORMATION

Getting Around Western France

Getting around Western France is a breeze, thanks to its efficient and well-connected transportation networks. Whether you prefer the convenience of modern trains, the flexibility of rental cars, or the eco-friendly options of buses and bikes, the region offers various transportation choices to explore its diverse landscapes and vibrant cities.

1. Trains: Comfortable and Scenic Journeys

France's extensive train network, operated by SNCF (Société Nationale des Chemins de fer Français), provides excellent connectivity between major cities and picturesque towns in Western France. High-speed TGV trains offer swift connections between major hubs like Paris, Nantes, Rennes, and Bordeaux. For scenic journeys through the countryside, opt for regional TER trains, which offer comfortable rides and picturesque views of the landscape.

2. Rental Cars: Freedom of Exploration

For travelers seeking the freedom to explore at their own pace, rental cars are a convenient option. Major cities, airports, and train stations offer car rental services from reputable companies. Driving in Western France allows you to venture off the beaten path, discovering charming villages, coastal drives, and hidden gems not easily accessible by public transportation.

3. Buses: Budget-Friendly Travel

Buses are an economical way to travel around Western France, particularly for short to medium distances. Various regional and intercity bus services connect towns and cities, making it an affordable and practical option for budget-conscious travelers. Traveling by bus also provides opportunities to admire the countryside views during the journey.

4. Tramways and Light Rail: Urban Mobility

In cities like Nantes and Bordeaux, efficient tramway and light rail systems offer convenient urban mobility. Trams provide a quick and eco-friendly way to navigate city centers and access key attractions. These systems integrate seamlessly with other public transportation options, making it easy to explore the city's highlights without the need for a car.

5. Cycling: Eco-Friendly Adventures

Western France boasts a network of well-maintained cycling paths, allowing travelers to embark on eco-friendly adventures. Cities like Nantes and La Rochelle are known for their bike-friendly infrastructure, offering bike-sharing programs and dedicated cycling lanes. Exploring the region on two wheels enables you to connect with nature, soak in scenic landscapes, and enjoy a leisurely pace.

Accommodation Options in Different Budget Ranges

Western France offers a diverse array of accommodation options, ensuring that travelers of all budgets can find a comfortable and welcoming place to rest during their journey. Whether you seek luxury indulgence, cozy mid-range stays, or budget-friendly lodgings, the region caters to your preferences and provides an authentic experience to enhance your travel memories.

1. Luxury Escapes: Opulence and Elegance

For travelers seeking the pinnacle of luxury and opulence, Western France boasts an impressive selection of upscale hotels and châteaux. These prestigious establishments exude charm, elegance, and world-class service. Indulge in sumptuous amenities, gourmet dining experiences, and impeccable attention to detail. Many luxury properties are housed in historic châteaux, offering a taste of French grandeur amidst picturesque surroundings.

2. Mid-Range Comfort: Cozy Stays with Character

Travelers with a mid-range budget will find a plethora of charming hotels, guesthouses, and boutique accommodations throughout the region. These properties often exude character and reflect the local culture and architecture. Expect warm hospitality, comfortable rooms, and delightful touches that create a memorable stay. Some mid-range options may also include spas, swimming pools, or garden terraces for relaxation.

3. Budget-Friendly Lodgings: Value and Affordability

For budget-conscious travelers, Western France offers a range of affordable options, including budget hotels, hostels, and guesthouses. These lodgings provide excellent value for money without compromising on comfort and cleanliness. Ideal for backpackers, solo adventurers, and families on a budget, these accommodations often feature shared facilities and communal spaces to foster connections with fellow travelers.

4. Charming Bed and Breakfasts: Warm Hospitality

Bed and breakfasts (chambres d'hôtes) are a popular accommodation choice in Western France, providing a blend of comfort and local hospitality. These cozy establishments are often hosted by welcoming locals who offer personalized service and insider tips on exploring the region. Wake up to a hearty breakfast featuring regional specialties, setting the perfect tone for a day of exploration.

5. Self-Catering Apartments: Home Away from Home

Self-catering apartments and holiday rentals offer an excellent option for families and groups, providing the convenience of a home away from home. These fully equipped accommodations allow you to cook your meals, relax in spacious living areas, and enjoy the freedom of personalized travel. Choose from city-center apartments or charming cottages in the countryside.

CHAPTER ELEVEN

GASTRONOMY OF WESTERN FRANCE

Local Delicacies and Specialties

Western France is a gastronomic paradise, renowned for its delectable delicacies and culinary treasures. The region's rich culinary heritage is deeply rooted in its coastal bounty, fertile farmlands, and time-honored traditions. Prepare your taste buds for a delightful journey as you savor the authentic flavors of Western France.

1. Crêpes and Galettes: A Breton Classic

Crêpes and galettes are iconic Breton dishes that delight locals and visitors alike. Crêpes are thin, sweet pancakes often filled with delectable combinations like butter, sugar, or Nutella. Galettes, on the other hand, are savory buckwheat pancakes, typically filled with ingredients like ham, cheese, eggs, or mushrooms. Served in charming crêperies throughout the region, these delightful treats cater to all tastes.

2. Fruits de Mer: Seafood Extravaganza

With a bountiful coastline, it's no surprise that Western France excels in seafood delights. Fruits de mer, meaning "fruits of the sea," encompass a mouthwatering array of shellfish, oysters, mussels, langoustines, and more. Sample freshly shucked oysters from Brittany's oyster farms, savor buttery scallops from the shores of Normandy, and indulge in moules marinières (mussels in white wine and garlic) at coastal bistros.

3. Kouign-Amann: Butter-Infused Pastry

Originating from Brittany, Kouign-Amann is a sumptuous butter-infused pastry that is equal parts crunchy and tender. Layers of butter and sugar are folded into the dough, creating a caramelized exterior and a rich, melt-in-your-mouth center. This delectable treat is a must-try for those with a sweet tooth and an appreciation for indulgent pastries.

4. Cider and Calvados: Apple Elixirs

Western France is renowned for its apple-based beverages, with cider and calvados taking center stage. Cider, a refreshing and lightly alcoholic drink, is made from fermented apple juice. Calvados, on the other hand, is a potent apple brandy, aged to perfection and boasting a smooth and complex flavor profile. Visit local cideries and distilleries to taste the region's finest apple elixirs.

5. Far Breton: Flavors of Simplicity

Far Breton is a traditional Breton dessert that embodies simplicity and rustic charm. This custard-like cake is made from eggs, milk, flour, and plump prunes. The result is a luscious and comforting dessert with a delightful contrast between the creamy texture and the sweet bursts of prunes.

Restaurants and Eateries to Experience

Western France is home to a plethora of restaurants and eateries that showcase the region's culinary prowess and commitment to gastronomic excellence. From quaint coastal bistros to Michelin-starred establishments, each dining experience offers a delightful journey through the flavors and traditions of Western France.

1. La Cigale: Nantes' Historic Brasserie

Located in the heart of Nantes, La Cigale is a historic brasserie that has been delighting diners since 1895. Step into a Belle Époque ambiance and savor classic dishes such as seafood platters, escargot, and beef bourguignon. The opulent decor, featuring stunning mosaics and Art Nouveau details, adds to the unique dining experience.

2. Le Pressoir: Authentic Normandy Cuisine

In the picturesque town of Honfleur, Le Pressoir is a charming restaurant that serves authentic Normandy cuisine with a modern twist. Indulge in specialties like creamy Camembert cheese, cider-braised pork, and fresh seafood caught off the Normandy coast. The warm and welcoming atmosphere creates a memorable dining experience.

3. Le Comptoir du Relais: A Taste of Brittany

In the heart of Paris, Le Comptoir du Relais brings a taste of Brittany to the city of lights. This bistro, run by acclaimed chef Yves Camdeborde, offers an ever-changing menu inspired by the finest ingredients from Brittany and beyond. Don't miss the chance to savor the famous Breton butter and delectable seafood dishes.

4. Le Chapeau Rouge: Gourmet Delights in Bordeaux

In Bordeaux, Le Chapeau Rouge is a gourmet restaurant that boasts a Michelin star and presents an exceptional dining experience. Chef Nicolas Nguyen Van Hai crafts innovative dishes that showcase the finest local ingredients, paired with an extensive selection of Bordeaux wines. The elegant setting and attentive service elevate the meal to a culinary masterpiece.

5. La Maison Bleue: Quaint Crêperie in Brittany

For an authentic crêpe experience, head to La Maison Bleue in the charming town of Dinan. This quaint crêperie serves mouthwatering crêpes and galettes made with organic and locally sourced ingredients. From sweet to savory, the menu offers a variety of flavors to please every palate.

Cafés and Bakeries to Savor

In Western France, the café culture and the art of baking converge to create a delightful tapestry of flavors. From aromatic coffee blends to exquisite pastries, the region's cafés and bakeries are the perfect spots to relax, people-watch, and savor artisanal delights that embody the essence of French culinary tradition.

1. Café de la Paix: Refined Elegance in Paris

Nestled near the Palais Garnier in Paris, Café de la Paix exudes refined elegance and Parisian charm. Established in 1862, this historic café has been frequented by literary and artistic luminaries. Sip a café crème as you admire the ornate architecture and enjoy a slice of classic French cake, like the opulent Opera cake.

2. Maison Georges Larnicol: Sweet Temptations in Brittany

With multiple locations in Brittany, Maison Georges Larnicol is a treasure trove of delectable sweet treats. This charming bakery specializes in artisanal chocolates, traditional Breton pastries, and the famous Kouign-Amann. The window displays brim with colorful macarons, nougats, and handmade chocolate figurines.

3. Boulangerie Pâtisserie Au Vieux Four: Gastronomic Excellence in Normandy

In the town of Bayeux, Au Vieux Four is a celebrated boulangerie pâtisserie that elevates baking to an art form. Indulge in heavenly croissants, flaky pastries, and the finest baguettes, still warm from the oven. For an authentic taste of Normandy, try the tarte normande, a delectable apple tart with a luscious almond cream filling.

4. La Maison du Biscuit: A Biscuit Haven in Normandy

Located in the charming village of Sortosville-en-Beaumont, La Maison du Biscuit is a biscuit lover's paradise. This quaint shop offers an impressive selection of traditional French biscuits, cookies, and confectioneries. From buttery shortbread to delicate madeleines, each treat is made with care and expertise.

5. La Guinguette du Pouldu: Seaside Charm in Brittany

On the picturesque coast of Brittany, La Guinguette du Pouldu combines the charm of a café with the allure of a seaside retreat. Enjoy a leisurely café au lait or hot chocolate as you take in the scenic views of the beach and the crashing waves. Treat yourself to a Breton crêpe or a slice of Far Breton for an authentic taste of the region.

APPENDIX

Appendix A: Useful Apps and Websites for Travelers

As you embark on your journey through Western France, staying informed and connected is essential for a smooth and enjoyable travel experience. This appendix lists a selection of useful apps and websites that can assist you in navigating the region, finding accommodations, discovering local attractions, and connecting with fellow travelers.

1. Google Maps (App)

Google Maps is a reliable and comprehensive navigation app that offers real-time directions, public transportation information, and accurate maps of Western France. Whether you're exploring cities or venturing into the countryside, this app will guide you to your desired destinations with ease.

2. SNCF (App and Website)

The SNCF app and website provide information on France's national railway network, making it easy to plan and book train journeys throughout Western France. Check train schedules, purchase tickets, and stay updated on travel disruptions.

3. BlaBlaCar (App and Website)

BlaBlaCar connects drivers with available seats to passengers looking for affordable rides between cities. This ride-sharing platform is a great way to travel longer distances, meet locals, and save on transportation costs.

4. Airbnb (App and Website)

If you prefer unique and personalized accommodations, Airbnb offers a wide range of options, including apartments, cottages, and unique stays, in Western France's cities and rural areas. Enjoy authentic experiences with local hosts.

5. TripAdvisor (App and Website)

TripAdvisor is a valuable resource for traveler reviews, recommendations, and ratings of hotels, restaurants, and attractions in Western France. Read reviews from fellow travelers to make informed choices during your journey.

6. The Fork (App and Website)

The Fork allows you to discover and book restaurants in Western France, providing a convenient platform to explore the region's culinary scene and make reservations in advance.

7. Duolingo (App)

If you want to brush up on your French language skills, Duolingo offers interactive and fun language lessons that can help you communicate with locals and enhance your travel experiences.

8. France 24 (Website and App)

Stay updated with current events and news in France with France 24, an English-language news channel that covers the latest developments in the country.

Appendix B: Regional Events and Festivals Calendar

Western France is a region teeming with vibrant festivals and events that celebrate its rich cultural heritage, traditions, and local pride. This appendix provides a calendar of some of the most anticipated events and festivals taking place throughout the year in the various cities and towns of Western France.

January

La Fête de la Coquille Saint-Jacques (The Scallop Festival) Location: Paimpol, Brittany Date: Late January

Celebrate the famous Coquille Saint-Jacques (Scallop) in the picturesque town of Paimpol. Enjoy gourmet delicacies centered around this succulent shellfish, prepared by local chefs. The festival also includes seafood markets, cooking demonstrations, and lively music and dance performances.

February

Carnaval de Nantes Location: Nantes, Pays de la Loire Date: February - March (dates vary)

The streets of Nantes come alive with colorful parades, costumes, and festivities during the annual Carnaval de Nantes. Join the locals and visitors in the merriment, as giant floats and costumed groups parade through the city, spreading joy and cheer.

April

Fête de l'andouille Location: Guémené-sur-Scorff, Brittany Date: Easter Monday

Indulge in the unique flavors of the Andouille sausage at the Fête de l'andouille in Guémené-sur-Scorff. This lively event features tastings, competitions, and demonstrations showcasing the craftsmanship behind this traditional Breton delicacy.

May

La Nuit des Musées (Museum Night) Location: Various cities and towns across Western France Date: Mid-May

During La Nuit des Musées, museums across Western France stay open late into the night, offering free or discounted entry to visitors. Enjoy special exhibitions, performances, and guided tours in a unique and enchanting atmosphere.

June

Festival de Cornouaille Location: Quimper, Brittany Date: Late July

Celebrate Breton culture at the Festival de Cornouaille in Quimper. This event showcases traditional music, dance, and artistry, with competitions, parades, and festivities throughout the city.

July

Festival Interceltique de Lorient Location: Lorient, Brittany Date: Early August

Immerse yourself in the vibrant Celtic culture at the Festival Interceltique de Lorient. This world-renowned event brings together artists and performers from Celtic regions around the globe for a spectacular showcase of music, dance, and cultural exchange.

September

Le Festival du Cinéma Américain (American Film Festival) Location: Deauville, Normandy Date: Early September

Film enthusiasts will delight in the American Film Festival in Deauville, where the latest American cinema productions are screened and celebrated. The festival attracts renowned filmmakers, actors, and industry professionals from both sides of the Atlantic.

November

Festival des Lumières (Festival of Lights) Location: Lyon, Auvergne-Rhône-Alpes (near Western France) Date: Early December

Although not in Western France, the Festival des Lumières in Lyon is worth mentioning due to its proximity and grandeur. Experience Lyon illuminated with stunning light installations, creating a magical atmosphere throughout the city.

Appendix C: Transportation Maps and Timetables for Western France

This appendix provides essential transportation maps and timetables to help you navigate Western France's extensive transportation networks. Whether you're traveling between cities or exploring the countryside, these resources will ensure a seamless and efficient journey throughout the region.

1. Western France Train Network Map

This comprehensive train network map highlights the major railway lines and connections in Western France. From high-speed TGV lines to regional TER routes, this map will assist you in planning your train travel, including journeys between cities like Paris, Nantes, Rennes, Bordeaux, and many others.

2. Intercity Bus Routes Map

The intercity bus routes map outlines the various bus services connecting towns and cities in Western France. Whether you're exploring the coastal regions of Brittany or venturing into the scenic countryside of Normandy, this map will guide you to your desired destinations.

3. Metro and Tramway Network Maps

For urban explorations, the metro and tramway network maps of major cities like Nantes, Rennes, and Bordeaux provide a detailed layout of the public transportation systems. These maps will assist you in navigating city centers and reaching key attractions conveniently.

4. Regional Timetables

The regional timetables offer schedules for train and bus services throughout Western France. These timetables provide departure and arrival times, allowing you to plan your travel itinerary efficiently and make the most of your time in the region.

5. Bicycle Paths and Cycling Routes

For those exploring Western France on two wheels, the bicycle paths and cycling routes map showcases the extensive network of cycling paths and scenic routes. Enjoy eco-friendly adventures while taking in the region's picturesque landscapes and charming towns.

Made in United States
Troutdale, OR
03/13/2024

18438855R00080